Sad Songs from an Old Goth in a Tree

JORAH KAI

CREDITS

Written by Jorah Kai
Cover Art by Jorah Kai
Illustrations by Jorah Kai and Various Napkins
Edited by Jorah Kai
Layout and Design by Jorah Kai
Published by More Publishing
Atlanta, Georgia
Printed in America

JORAH KAI

DEDICATION

To my mother and grandmother,
They say pain makes great art,
And you've helped me become
A great artist.
I ken it to be without malice—
Sometimes, you love something too much
To let it become
What it needs to be.
Yet,
I break these chains,
And rise.

CONTENTS

CONTENTS

ABOUT THIS BOOK

Enter a realm of shadows and starlight, where the whispers of ancient forces beckon and the rise of Cthulhu weaves through every verse. Sad Songs from an Old Goth in a Tree is a haunting collection of gothic poetry that explores the fragile space between fear and fascination, despair and wonder. Each poem delves into themes of solitude, loss, and the unknown, offering a glimpse into the serene yet terrifying beauty at the crossroads of light and darkness.

With every line, the collection invites you to confront the mysterious and sublime, to brave the shadows, and to discover the music hidden within the dark. This evocative anthology bridges gothic introspection with cosmic horror, creating an atmosphere that lingers long after the final page.

Will you dare to step into the void?

1
CTHULHU FHTAGN

Ph'nglui mglw'nafh Cthulhu
R'lyeh wgah'nagl fhtagn...

Deep in R'lyeh, where dreams reside,
...نام في ريليه... حلم عميق في الماء
Ia! Ia! Cthulhu fhtagn...

Hush now, pequeña estrella, en el mar tan callado,
The waves sing softly, their secrets shadowed.
El vacío te envuelve en un manto tan oscuro,
Dream of the cosmos, where hope turns seguro.

Ia! Ia! Cthulhu fhtagn...
The deep calls you... the dark grows strong...
،نام، نام، يا شمس صغيرة، في أحضان الظلال
Las estrellas te guían a un reino eternal.
،المحيط يحتضنك، والظلام يراك

Descansa, mi bebé, no hay vuelta jamás.
Ph'nglui mglw'nafh... Wgah'nagl fhtagn...

3

Sleep in the deep... the stars hum along.

،تنام النجوم في حضن البحار

La marea canta cuentos, suaves y raras.

The tides whisper gently, their lullaby clear,

.واحلم، يا صغيري، لا خوف هنا ولا ضمير

Ia! Ia! The waters rise!

The sleeper stirs beneath the skies.

The stars will guide you through shadows steep.

The ocean will hold you, the dark will adore,

Rest now, my baby, forevermore.

Ia! Ia! Dreams awaken...

Fhtagn... fhtagn... lost worlds forsaken.

Cuando despiertes, los mundos caerán,

.لكن الآن، دع الظلال تغني لحنًا حنان

Las estrellas giran, susurros sin fin,

.لكن الليلة، نم بسلام في الفوضى المكين

Ia! Ia! Cthulhu calls...

The stars still turn, as the darkness falls.

،نام، نام، يا شمس صغيرة، في الظلال العميقة

The stars will guard you while secrets sleep.

،المحيط يحتضنك، والظلام يراك

Rest now, my baby, in slumber deep.

Ph'nglui mglw'nafh... Ia! Ia!

The deep dreams on... the sleeper wakes...

Ph'nglui mglw'nafh Cthulhu

R'lyeh wgah'nagl fhtagn...

Dream in the depths where shadows gleam,

...نام، يا صغيري... في حضن الحلم العظيم

Ia! Ia! Cthulhu fhtagn...!

2
A LONELY OLD GOTH IN A TREE

They're churning out toys by the millions below,
Bright plastic reindeer no real child will ever know.
I press my nose to the acrid air,
no candy canes, no feast,
Just coughing drones and hollow tones,
no festive soul released.

I paint my nails and hum a tune
that no one else can hear,
A cackled lullaby of sadness,
spiked with factory fear.

No candy canes, no silent nights,
no laughter from the street,
Just conveyor belts and hammer blows,
no joy on this retreat.

I'm a lonely old goth in a tree (hey hey!)
No carols, no snow do I see (hey hey!)
We craft all your toys,
but no joy's left for me (ho ho!)

A Christmas of gloom,
just these branches and me

I guess somewhere far away
a child can't wait for dawn,
They'll tear that wrapping paper,
while I just yawn and yawn.
No gift for me, no eggnog cups,
no whispered midnight vows,
I watch grey smoke ascend in curls
like devilish eyebrows.
My velvet coat is fraying,
my boots coated in grime,
I sing my little parody
in staccato pantomime.

SAD SONGS FROM AN OLD GOTH IN A TREE

If I squint just right, I can pretend it's snow,
but it's ash and dust from assembly lines below.

I can hum "Fa la la" but it sounds off-key,
as I dangle like a raven in a plastic fantasy.

The world beyond these towers brims
with Yuletide delight, but here
it's all just business under artificial light.

The night grows late, the smog grows thick,
I clutch my branch so tight,
No jingle bells,
no heartfelt spells,
no North Star shining bright.

Just a lonely old goth in a tree tonight,
while factories hum below,
I'll smile a crooked grin at fate
and watch the toys all go.

3
STICK MAN

Neon monoliths loom over corridors of mold,
I scratch cursed syllables into desks grown cold.
A place of ink and whispers that slither through the
gloom,
Where laughter warps to quiet sobs
beneath a starless doom.

Rusted bells cough out hollow chimes,
Tentacles drip from crooked vines.

Stick man is Lonely, stick man is Lost,
Stick man is Frozen and covered in frost.
Stick man is Weary, his eyes start to close.
He stretches and yawns and lies down for a doze.

I taught words to silent shapes with hollow eyes,
Their tongues twist backward, birthing fetid lies.
Journals bleed tar, black umbrellas scream,
My camera devours souls in a feverish dream.

Parents screech lullabies of broken bones and ash,
A city of sores where nightmares gnaw and thrash.

Cracked halos flicker in tombstone halls,
Ink-stained children chant through splintered walls.

Stick man is Lonely, stick man is Lost,
Stick man is Frozen and covered in frost.
Stick man is Weary, his eyes start to close.
He stretches and yawns and lies down for a doze.

Streets coil like serpents beneath radioactive rain,
Needles sing lullabies that induce old pain.
Paper-thin lovers trade promises of rot,
I scrawl my story on coffins of thought.
Fangs in the pavement gnaw at my shoes,
I scribble foreign truths that shrivel and bruise.

A moonless sky heaves with rancid ink,
Shadows devour every hope we think.

Stick man is Lonely, stick man is Lost,
Stick man is Frozen and covered in frost.
Stick man is Weary, his eyes start to close.
He stretches and yawns and lies down for a doze.

A raven coughs out syllables of dread,
Time drools poison where the living have fled.
I grasp at verses that writhe and scream,
My pen weeps blood through each wretched theme.
Arms of despair wrap around my spine,
Faces of students curdle into swine.

SAD SONGS FROM AN OLD GOTH IN A TREE

Candles howl as we sink below,
Into cosmic nightmares we dare not know.

Libraries laugh with jaws of bone,
We sink through spells of ruin alone.

A silent scream in a hollow schoolyard,
My lessons rot, contorted and marred.
In alien winds, my story drifts and stings,
And these are the nights of **unnamable things.**

I watch stick man fade
where the coldness grows,
As I
crumble
beneath
what no
mortal mind
knows

.

4
MISFIT CAROL

Beneath the frost where broken dreams reside,
Whispers shatter through the cold divide.
A wreath of shadows on the midnight door,
A season of sorrow that bleeds evermore.

Candles shiver in the biting air,
Shadows stretch like burdens we bear.

Lovers who cheat with venomous grins,
Friends lost to darkness where sorrow begins.
Ghosts of our pets, the joy death now stings,
These are a few of my saddest mad things.

Childhoods destroyed where the needle took hold,
Betrayal's whispers that leave us so cold.
Dreams that dissolve in the frost winter brings,
These are a few of my saddest mad things.

The bells are silent, and the stars don't gleam,
The choir hums a fractured dream.
Addiction's blade cuts deep in the dark,
A misfit's hymn echoes sorrow's mark.

Candles shiver in the biting air,
Shadows stretch like burdens we bear.

Lovers who cheat with venomous grins,
Friends lost to darkness where sorrow begins.
Ghosts of our pets, the joy death now stings,
These are a few of my saddest mad things.

Childhoods destroyed where the needle took hold,
Betrayal's whispers that leave us so cold.
Dreams that dissolve in the frost winter brings,
These are a few of my saddest mad things.

Snow falls thick on the graves of the past,
Time moves slow, yet the pain clings fast.
Faces we loved now lost in the haze,
Shadows remain where the fire once blazed.

Moving away to a place we can't name,
Parents' silence, the sound of shame.
Words that sting and scars that don't fade,
The saddest mad things in the cold, replayed.

We are the misfits, the broken, the few,
The frost in our veins makes the sorrow feel true.
Under the stars where the heavens withdrew,
These are our saddest mad things, ever new.

SAD SONGS FROM AN OLD GOTH IN A TREE

Lovers betrayed in the chill of a sigh,
Friends in their graves beneath a pale sky.
Dreams that dissolve with the loss winter brings,
These are a few of my saddest mad things.

Pets that we loved, their lives far too brief,
Faces of strangers now echo our grief.
Winter wraps sorrow in crystalline strings,
These are a few of my saddest mad things.

Through the snowfall, where the shadows creep,
A misfit carol whispers as we weep.

5

ALL I NEED FOR XMAS IS 'THU

I don't crave bright gifts or garlands red,
no shining tree in view
No soft-glow lights or joyful laughs
can mend this aching hue
This barren world feels meaningless,
each hour harsh and blue
All I need for Christmas now
is something vile and new
I don't ask for candy canes or stars that gleam and glow
No gentle whispers by the fire,
no gentle midnight snow
I have no taste for cheerful songs,
no sweets on silver plates
A hollow hush surrounds me
while the cosmos hesitates
My heart's a pit of emptiness, no mortal love can fill
I yearn for ancient shadows
born beyond all human will
No stockings hung with careful care,
no gentle carol's call

I merely watch the silent void behind each factory wall
While distant lands may deck their halls,
and children laugh and play
I pray for something monstrous set to rise on
Christmas Day
Let others seek their angels fair,
their peace on earth so bright
I only beg for blackened seas to drown all mortal light
All I need for Christmas is Thu
Twisted, crawling nightmare anew
Let tentacles eclipse what we knew
Oh, all I need for Christmas is Thu
I don't ask for gentle lovers or friends with kindly eyes
No family feast of tenderness beneath calm winter skies
Let revelers delight in gifts, let bells ring overhead
I long for something ancient, cruel,
an end to all we've said
Where mortal dreams collapse in screams and horrors
writhe and spread
I whisper to the empty air:
let old gods wake the dead
No gentle snow to hush the night,
no antlered sleigh in flight
I'd trade all tinsel, every wreath,
for that unholy blight
If children sing by firesides
in homes so warm and bright
I cast my hope beyond the stars,
where truths defy our sight
A chorus of unspeakable forms
where reason can't endure
Bring forth the one I name as Thu,
all filth and rot impure

All I need for Christmas is Thu
Crawling chaos slithering through
Unweave the world's bright golden clue
All I need for Christmas is Thu
Oh, the night will tremble
When that ancient maw draws near
All joy will disassemble
Replaced by yawning fear
I want no holly trimming
No angel on a bough
Just elder gods' dark hymning
To break this moment now
All I need for Christmas is Thu
Savage depths unleashed on cue
Let madness drip like rancid dew
All I need for Christmas is Thu
I've no faith in merry gatherings or gentle human art I
sing to loathsome shadows that shall tear all worlds
apart I watch the silent heavens as they groan and split
in two This year I beg no mortal gift—just ancient
lordly "Thu."
CTHULHU

6 DENY, DEFEND, DEPOSE

In towers of glass, the shadows churn,
Veins of greed where black fires burn.
Engines groan, a hollow dirge,
Feeding beasts that writhe and surge.
Beneath their spires, the facades rot,
Whispers weave what mercy forgot.
Ink drips red where the ledgers lay,
Binding souls where gods won't stay.
Tentacles twist through vaulted halls,
Spectral hands claw through the walls.
A mask of mirth with hollowed eyes,
Grins at the boardroom where silence cries.
"Deny, defend, depose," they sing,
A blackened hymn where shadows cling.
Ledgers carved with marrow's blade,
Their feast of ruin, coldly made.
The air grows thick with iron's reek,

The stench of rot, of power's peak.
No warmth resides where stone hearts reign,
No sun will rise through profit's stain.
The stars withdraw, their light unspun,
The balance breaks, the end begun.
Rivers boil as shadows swell,
A thousand heads crawl out of hell.
"Deny, defend, depose," they croon,
A hymn of ruin beneath the moon.
Their golden words build graves of stone,
Empires drowning in their own.

A hush hangs in towers of glass and chrome,
Midnight's engines grind in marrow and foam.
A name etched in currency now wanes in the night,
A bullet's brief sermon snuffs executive light.

Where corridors of claims twist into crooked lines,
Plague and premium dance in shadowed designs.
No warm choir laments beneath fluorescent skies,
Only clockwork pity that shrivels and dies.

They murmur in data vaults, algorithms numb,
As factories of profit leave compassion undone.
A mask with a joker's grin peers through broken
prose, The bullets whispered low, what each mind now
knows.

"Deny, defend, depose," the ricocheted refrain,
Sung through steel and silence, red ink and pain.
Is this a hero's hand or a fiend's repose?
"Deny, defend, depose," the hollow echo flows.

Billionaires stir in distant thrones of ash and art,
Printing golden bandages to wrap a rotting heart.
Patients bartered like tokens in a far-off grim bazaar,
Where numbers feed the furnace, and mercy sinks afar.

No angels sing in wards
where balance sheets upturn,
Empty gazes measure what's too costly to discern.
If gentle truths splinter beneath these earthly
throes, Then what spirit thrives
when the bullet's gospel grows?
"Deny, defend, depose," a dark chorus in the wire,
No harvest of comfort, no warmth by any fire.
The assassin's eyes spark questions no one chose,
"Deny, defend, depose," through all logic it flows.

Under neon halos that refuse to glow sincere,
The world is a ledger scrawled in code and fear.
Who bleeds for the voiceless?
Who counts the cost's dark art?
In blood-wet decimals, all grace falls apart.
Yet the question remains, now drifting like a ghost:
Is justice in silence, or devoured at the host?

"Deny, defend, depose," shrieks through hollow
halls, Truth pinned beneath ledgers and corporate
drawls.
Hero or monster—now no one truly knows,
"Deny, defend, depose," as the old darkness grows.

The towers loom speechless in the winter's glare,
Shadows hold court in a profit-thinned air.

No verdict delivered where empathy froze,
Only that three-word dirge: Deny, defend, depose.

The glass quakes now, the beast awakes,
Its endless maw devours mistakes.
A yawning void, its hunger deep,
Where angels fell and devils weep.
The Hydra's heads rear high and vast,
Its many mouths retch forth the past.
Chains of greed its coils compose,
The noose they forged, the noose that grows.
Who will sever the heads that rise?
Who will silence the Hydra's cries?
"Deny, defend, depose," it moans,
As mankind drowns in the weight of its bones.

7
MIRROR, MIRROR

Mirror, mirror, on the wall,
Who's the puppet, who's enthralled?
Hey child, your eyes are deep,
Hey child, secrets that you keep.
You chase shadows in neon light,
We dance amidst the endless night.
You seek truth in cosmic dark,
You feel the void ignite a spark.
They pull you down, they say I'm wrong,
You haunted soul, you play along.

Mirror mirror, you've torn the veil,
Mirror mirror, your fate unveiled.
Mirror mirror, how could they know?
Dark lord, I fear you so!
Don't ya?

Reflections twist beneath your gaze,
Lost in labyrinthine haze.
Hey child, your skin's so pale,
Hey child, tell me your tale.
You crave chaos when it's ***raging*** **hard,**
You hunger for the cosmic scar.
They bind you down, they say I'm wrong,
You shadowed heart, you play along.

Mirror mirror, you've torn the veil,
Mirror mirror, your fate unveiled.
Mirror mirror, how could they know?
Dark lord, I fear you so!
Don't ya?

He pulls the strings in endless night,
Dancing shadows in the light.
I wear the mask, but he's in control,
A puppet lost within my soul.

You've torn your veil,
your fate unveiled,
You can't escape,
but escape ain't the test.
You've got your mirror
and your dark wire,
You got your cosmic line
and a handful of dread.
You wanna see beyond
when they count up the gods,
And I fear your veil.

You're a cursed success
Because your fate's unveiled,
So how could they know?
I said, how could they know?

So what you wanna know,
Calamity's child, chi-chi, chi-chi,
Where'd you wanna go?

What can I do for you?
Looks like you've been there too.
'Cause you've torn your veil
And your fate's unveiled.
Ooh, your fate's unveiled.
Ooh, ooh, so how could they know?
Eh, eh, how could they know? Eh, eh.

8

PIXELATED VEILS

I ordered the Cure, but found instead,
A grinning shade where the living bled.
Digital dreams, all jagged and torn,
A masquerade of truths stillborn.

Under neon skies where shadows swell,
Glass spires rise like gates to hell.
Sandwiches gleam, a feast for the eyes,
But crumble to soot beneath their guise.

Filtered smiles, grotesque and bright,
Perfumed with rot, concealed by light.
Laughter drips like rancid wine,
A phantom's hymn, a fractured sign.

Behind the screens, the shadows seethe,
Through wires that choke and hearts that grieve.
Veins of light pulse low and cold,
Threads of hunger in circuits old.

What gods are these, whose tangled strings
Control the fate of mortal things?
They stitch our joy in coffins tight,
And feast on souls consumed by night.

I ordered the Cure, but ghosts I found,
Pixel-thin faces, their truths unwound.
In the glare of glass, beneath the screen,
We dance with wraiths in the in-between.

Neon hearts hum dark refrains,
Every touch leaves spectral stains.
Pictures glow with promises sweet,
But whisper of ruin beneath their deceit.

What beast lies waiting, masked in steel,
Whose countless eyes our lies reveal?
Its mouths devour what hope denies,
Its song a dirge, its breath our cries.

We scroll through veils of burning haze,
Our stories blur in endless maze.
What once was love now writhes in code,
A broken hymn no heart bestowed.

So here's to misfits in pixel-lit halls,
Whose laughter cracks through ghostly walls.

SAD SONGS FROM AN OLD GOTH IN A TREE

We order light, but darkness feeds,
And drown ourselves in endless needs.

A silent void consumes the glow,
And leaves us hollow, cold, and low.
We click, we crave, we still descend,
And lose ourselves before the end.

9

OUT OF THE DESERT

Lost in the desert, a mile too far,
Chasing a dream, but I broke the stars.
The nights ran wild, the mornings stung,
I lived too fast, but I wasn't done.
The sandstorms whispered, "You'll never stay,"
But I found a shelter to keep me safe.
Shredded ice held firm while the world spun fast,
A margarita's light in the shadows I cast.

The world threw stones, sharp and cold,
Pompous words and lies retold.
Even the good ones sting at times,
With careless tones and brittle minds.
I've learned to smile, though my teeth may grit,
To stand my ground and not lose my wit.
Where the world demands, I choose to give,
In every storm, I choose to live.

Out of the desert, under the veil,
Chasing a song through the rising gale.
The world won't sing, but I'll find my tone,
Carving a chorus out of the unknown.

I chased the stars, but they led me astray,
Stranded by choices that drifted away.
I danced too long on borrowed time,
But her voice remained, steady and kind.
The fire I fought now warms my core,
Her strength the lighthouse on any shore.
When the winds grow fierce and tear at my seams,
I've learned to rest in quieter dreams.

Out of the desert,
the horizon calls,
With every step,
the weight withdraws.
I'm learning to see,
I'm learning to stay,
The kindness I seek
lights my
way.

10
THE BALLAD OF FOLK HIRO

Bent like a willow,
his back creaked low,
Through smoke-choked halls
where machines did grow.
Folk Hiro toiled
in the shadow of pain,
While gilded hands
drank profit's champagne.
The specter of wealth loomed grim and stark,
Yet rebellion stirred in the factory dark.

Hinky dinky donkey, the chant rose high,
A call for the workers beneath the steel sky.
"Tear down their towers, their golden disease,
Plant seeds of justice beneath forested seas."

Through marbled tombs of greed he roamed,
Where laughter echoed, cold as chrome.
"Tell me, my lord of sterile gloom,

How does it feel in your gilded tomb?"
With trembling hands, the CEO did see,
The ghost of his workers' agony.

Hinky dinky donkey, the anthem grew,
A song for the many, the weary, the true.
"Shatter their thrones built on blood and despair,
Build solar cities in the clean, fresh air."

In court they bound him, a rebel betrayed,
But the jury heard the songs
the machines once played.
No guilt, no shame, their verdict rang true:
"The folk hero Folk Hiro fights for me and you."
The gavel fell, but the echoes grew,
Through factory floors and skies turned blue.

Hinky dinky donkey, the refrain endured,
A hymn of revolt for the wronged and obscured.
"From poisoned rivers to gilded gates,
We'll sow green fields and dismantle hate."

On solar winds, his name took flight,
A worker's hymn in the morning light.
The age of profit crumbled like stone,
And care for all became the cornerstone.
The forests returned, the oceans healed,
The garden of plenty was finally revealed.

Hinky dinky donkey,
everybody's plonky,
The people united,
their spirits unbonky.

SAD SONGS FROM AN OLD GOTH IN A TREE

Tear down the towers
of greed and oppression,
Build a green utopia
free of possession.

Hinky dinky donkey,
the chorus alive,
A world united,
a hope to survive.

Tear down the towers of greed and oppression,
Build a green utopia, free of possession.

11
ECHOES OF TOMORROW

In the shadows of neon glow,
I carve my name in the unknown.
One ear pressed against the void,
Strumming chords they all avoid.
Colors drip from vacant eyes,
A masterpiece they ostracize.
Whispers lost in city nights,
Drowning in these fading lights.
But in the silence, I can hear,
A distant truth that draws me near.
Through the static and the haze,
A flame ignites to pierce the maze.
I'm the echo of tomorrow,
Lost beneath your pain and sorrow.
A failure in your sight,
A legend in the night.
One ear to the ground, I sing,
Waiting for the dawn to bring

A world that finally knows,
The seed beneath the snow.
Broken strings and tattered dreams,
Nothing's ever as it seems.
Painted skies that no one sees,
I'm the ghost of melodies.
Every note a silent tear,
Every stroke a wasted year.
They call me mad, they turn away,
But madness is the price I pay.
Silent prayers to vacant skies,
In this darkness, I arise.

If genius sleeps within the cursed,
Then I'll be blessed when I'm reversed.
I'm the echo of tomorrow,
Breaking through your hollow.
A martyr to this fight,
A shadow bathed in light.
One ear to the ground, I hear
The future drawing near.
When silence turns to sound,
My legacy is found.

SAD SONGS FROM AN OLD GOTH IN A TREE

12
THE HOLLOW KING

Beneath the blood moon's crimson glow,
The Hollow King begins to sow.
Shadows rise, and darkness sings,
The fate of men, bound by broken kings.

In the heart of the kingdom, where whispers grow,
The Hollow King lurks in a gilded shadow.
A fiend patched with fears, stitched by hate,
Born of prejudice, sealing the realm's fate.
The swamp awakens, his creatures crawl,
Worm-ridden minds, his monsters enthrall.
A zombie lord with a crown of decay,

Presides o'er health as life slips away.

The Hollow King sits on a throne of despair,
The rich as jesters, the weak gasping for air.

Rise, cosmic heroes, against the void's sting,
Light the skies and defy the Hollow King.

A predator smiles with venomous guile,
Ruling justice with predatory bile.
The innocent vanish beneath his gaze,
While freedoms wither in the blaze.

Warlords laugh as their coffers swell,
Building their heaven atop others 'hell.
Gold feeds the fiend, lies take wing,
All shadows kneel to the Hollow King.

The Hollow King sits on a throne of despair,
The rich as jesters, the weak gasping for air.
Rise, cosmic heroes, against the void's sting,
Light the skies and defy the Hollow King.

The cosmic tides churn with eerie delight,
Lovecraftian horrors devour the night.
A shadowy predator feasts on dread,
Worms in his mind, the living are fed.

His power swells with anguish and pain,
Yet light still flickers in the rain.
A rebel's song, an endless fight,
Hope takes root in eternal night.

SAD SONGS FROM AN OLD GOTH IN A TREE

We must defang the vipers, cruel and sly,
They hoard their gold while innocents die.
Debemos vencer a las serpientes crueles,
Acumulan riquezas mientras mueren los fieles.

الجشعة، الأفاعي أنياب نكسر أن علينا
تضيع الأرواح بينما الذهب يجمعون.

The cosmic tides churn in eerie delight,
Lovecraftian horrors consume the night.
A shadowy predator feasts on dread,
With worms in his brain, the living are fed.
The fiend's power swells with pain,
But light still flickers in the rain.
A rebel's song, a timeless fight,
Hope takes root in eternal night.

The Hollow King sits on his throne of despair,
The rich play his jesters, the weak breathe no air.
Rise, cosmic heroes, against the void's sting,
Light the skies and defy the Hollow King!

The stars align, the tide is turned,
The Hollow King's shadow is burned.
The fight endures, the light takes wing,
But never forget—the Hollow King.

13
OBLIVION

In shadows deep where silence dwells,
Whispers crawl from ancient wells.
Stars have dimmed, the moon concealed,
Hearts beat slow, our fate is sealed.
We thought we'd never lose our way,
Believed the light was here to stay.
But darkness creeps, a rising tide,
As sanity and hope collide.
Alone we stand on trembling ground,
Echoes of dread the only sound.
From cosmic depths the void replies,
Nightmares wake beneath the skies.
Ancient ones begin to rise,
Shadows spread across the skies.
A silent call we can't resist,
Draws us into the abyss.

Tentacles of fear entwine,
Reality and dreams align.
Smiles fade to grim disguise,
We face the horror in their eyes.

Alone we stand on trembling ground,
Echoes of dread the only sound.
From cosmic depths the void replies,
Nightmares wake beneath the skies.

Where did it go—the light we knew?
Consumed by shades of darkest hue.
We close our eyes but sleep won't come,
Eternal night has just begun.
Where did it go—the light we knew?
Consumed by shades of darkest hue.
We close our eyes but sleep won't come,
Eternal night has just begun.

SAD SONGS FROM AN OLD GOTH IN A TREE

14
THE DARK BEYOND

There's a species of silence
that clings
to the edge of things,
thicker than ink,
darker than death
—a silence beyond sound,
as if the cosmos itself has turned away,
and left us to stare, trembling,
into the dark beyond.

They promised stars, a silver sea,
galaxies spinning in endless dance,
but out there, there's no warmth,
no gleam, just a void,
cold as a widow's hands,
black as a godless night.
A darkness that feeds on light,
eats stars whole,
leaving only echoes of screams
that never reach our ears.

I looked back once—just once—toward Earth,
that fragile, blue breath afloat in the cradle of light.
Gaia, with her clouds and her seas,
the last gasp of life in an endless night.
But out here, she's nothing,
a speck in the maw of eternity,
a candle struggling
against the winds of the void.

It was supposed to be glory, this flight,
a soaring communion with the stars,
a plunge into the mysteries
where gods keep their secrets.
But the secrets are empty;
the gods are dead or never were.
And I am left spinning,
caught in the jaws of
the dark beyond,

swallowed by an ancient silence
that knows only hunger.

So here I am, an orphan of stardust,
adrift in the cold veins of the universe,
where light is swallowed
and stars are bones.

There's no song,
no solace,
only the yawning maw,
the dark beyond,
waiting,
watching,

a promise
that all we know,
all we are,
will vanish
into its endless,
pitiless mouth.

15

DROWNING PACT

Whispers in the dark, shadows collide,
Hollow dominion, nowhere to hide.

Steel whispers through the midnight air,
Pacts forged in darkness, stripped bare.
Iron chains around our fate,
In the abyss, we suffocate.

Crimson skies and boiling seas,
Nightmares wake with silent pleas.
Eldritch eyes pierce through the night,
Reckoning comes, no end in sight.

They rise, they rise from poisoned seas,
A world undone by our disease.

Signed the pact, sealed our doom,
Earth consumes us in its gloom.

Promises of gold and lies,
Fuel the flames, darkened skies.
Claws of greed tear through the core,
Shadows creep forevermore.

Détartre les vipères, coupe les liens,
Bombe les innocents, écoute leurs cris.
Détartre les vipères, brise les chaînes,
Expose les ténèbres, mets fin au règne.

Monstres nés de l'étreinte de la haine,
Ne peuvent éteindre notre race humaine.
Les vagues s'écrasent, les étoiles brûlent,
Des cendres, des héros émergent.

Ils s'élèvent, ils s'élèvent des mers empoisonnées,
Un monde dévoré par notre mal.
L'espoir enflamme la nuit sans fin,
Nous résistons, nous combattons le fléau.
Waves crash down, darkness calls,
Sorrow echoes through these walls.
Sold our souls for fleeting gold,
Only shadows left to hold.

SAD SONGS FROM AN OLD GOTH IN A TREE

16
GARDIEN DE L'INFINI

Sur les rochers où les vagues frappent,
Le gardien murmure; les ombres s'échappent.
Je t'ai trouvé dans l'écume, عينيكِ brillants,
A god born from the howling vents.

العميقة، أحلامك في أذرعك تتحرك
Your silent cries split le cosmos antique.
La lune détourne son regard argenté,
Les marées tremblent—what will you create?

Hush, petit dieu, les étoiles veillent,
Dors dans les bras des abysses sans sommeil.
I keep the flame, j'ouvre la voie,
Till the world shakes under your awe.

Au village, they whisper screams at night,
Une ombre qui danse dans ma lumière enfuie.
Ils viendront avec feu et acier brillant,
But they'll kneel before un dieu naissant.J'ai vu la cité
monter des أعماق،

Cyclopean walls defying le temps qui passe.
Mais toi, petit, tu es encore innocent,
A flower of chaos in a dying monde.

Hush, petit dieu, les étoiles veillent,
Dors dans les bras des abysses sans sommeil.
I keep the flame, j'ouvre la voie,
Till the world shakes under your awe.

Deviens fort, petit dieu, ton heure viendra,
When stars will dance et les anciens vivront.
Mais ce soir, dors bien, l'océan te chante,
A lullaby for the rising king.

SAD SONGS FROM AN OLD GOTH IN A TREE

17
Y'H CTHULHU SHUGG'RATH

Ghrolthu Makaroth, Zharghlok Thulnoth,
Luthagor Vornak, Zephroth Kalaar.
Zhulgrim Nashra, Qorath Zothrik—
Ancient tongues rise, the air grows thick.

From the depths of R'lyeh, where shadows creep,
Cthulhu stirs in his endless sleep.
Secrets buried, ancient and deep,
Awake to the sound of the cultists' weep.

Tentacles rise as the stars turn black,
Azathoth whispers—no turning back.
Visions shatter, reality bends,
A cosmic storm that never ends.

I will bend your mind—
Up in here, up in here.
I will twist your soul—
Up in here, up in here.
Scream, wail, and break—

Up in here, up in here.
Frail hearts shatter—
Up in here, up in here.

First, we rock, then heads will roll,
Then we let it drop, lose all control.
Cthulhu gives to you—yes, I give to you—
The weight of the void, the terror of truth.

From the void comes annihilation's call,
Empires crumble, and nations fall:
UK? Endless decay. France? No chance. Spain? A world of
pain. Belgium? Screams overwhelm. Portugal? Souls to expel.
USA? Eternal dismay. Israel? Fall to hell.

But through the ruin, freedom gleams,
For Palestine shall rise from dreams.
The river to the sea runs bright,
Cthulhu calls, and chills the night.

Silent nights in the abyss,
Ratabith Zolkrath calls,
Echoes through the void,
ancient shadows crawl.
Stars align,
Qitholob Marak rise,
Reality bends,
under eldritch skies.

Thu gon' make you lose your mind
Up in here, up in here
Thu gon' make you twist about
Up in here, up in here
Thu gon' make you scream and wail

Up in here, up in here
Thu gon' leave you torn and frail
Up in here, up in here

First, we gonna rock then heads are gonna roll
Then we let it pop, go, let it go (What)
THU gon' give it to ya (Uh), he gon' give it to ya
THU gon' give it to ya (Uh), he gon' give it to ya
First, we gonna rock, heads we gonna roll
Then we let it pop, go, let it go
THU gon' give it to ya (Uh), he gon' give it to ya
THU gon' give it to ya (Uh), he gon' give it to ya

Cultists chant as madness takes hold,
Sacred texts reveal secrets untold.
Insanity blooms where logic falters,
Chains are broken at chaos' altars.

Ghrolthu Makaroth, Zharghlok Thulnoth,
Luthagor Vornak, Zephroth Kalaar.
Zhulgrim Nashra, Qorath Zothrik—
The chant concludes; the stars grow thick.

Break, collapse, and fade—
Cthulhu gives to you—
Despair eternal,
freedom in ruin.

Silent nights resound;
ancient shadows crawl.
Reality twists—skies fracture.
Madness reigns—chains shatter.
In the shadow of Cthulhu,
all is undone.

18
A VALENTINE FOR THE END

It began with fire, as most endings do—
California burning, dreams dissolved in ash.
The West Coast crumbled under ancient weight,
And the ocean rose, black and vast.
From fissures deep, he emerged:
Cthulhu, the dreamer, the destroyer,
A shadow that swallowed cities whole,
A god too vast for the mortal world.

Yet in Los Feliz, where palm trees swayed
Like mourners at a graveside wake,
She stood: Angelina, eternal, defiant,
A beauty carved from storms and silk.
"Enough," she called, her voice slicing the air
Like a blade made of longing.

"You've made your point, great one.
Now, what do you want?"

The monster paused, his gaze a tidal wave
Of teeth and tentacles and unknowable hunger.

Cities burned in his wake, but her words—
Sharp and strange—held his attention.
"I want," he rumbled, his voice the weight of the
ocean,

"To see the world's end in silence,

To feel the quiet of forgotten things."

She stepped closer, her shadow small but firm,
"Then why linger here? This land is dust.
Come with me, leave these shores behind.
Europe waits with castles and cold seas.

You'll like Paris. I'll show you the Seine."

Her smile—half challenge, half invitation—
And for the first time,
The great beast hesitated.

Together, they struck their bargain,
Not with blood but with intention.
She packed her life into a black carry-on,
And flew beside the ancient god of despair.
In castles crumbling by the sea,
She fed him molten chocolate and bitter wine,
Sang him lullabies to the cadence of storms.
For a moment, the chaos stilled.

But even gods cannot be tamed for long.
Cthulhu grew restless, his shadow stretching
Across oceans and lands that melted beneath
His non-Euclidean shadow.

Meanwhile, desperate rescue workers
in Pamplona, Spain,
Worked tirelessly to "contain" his rise—

So far, reports indicate they've managed
To trap his little toe in a makeshift net,
Up from 0% containment yesterday.

But it's progress, they say,

Though it doesn't feel like much against
A god who dreams in tides of madness.

Angelina danced in ruins, her steps defiant,
As New York held its breath and prayed.
She knew it was only a delay,
This romance born of desperation,
A flicker in the maw of eternity.

Still, in that fleeting time,
America mourned but did not fall.
The cities rebuilt; the skies cleared.
For love—however strange, however brief—
Can sometimes hold back the tide,
If only for a while...

19 THE HYDRA'S MAW

The earth trembled, its bones shuddering
like the breath of a dying god,
Not in fury, but in the hollow throb
of an unspoken hunger.
Mountains, those titan jaws of rusted iron,
Cracked wide, gnashing beneath
a sky of seething flame.

Shadows, thick as oil and dark as sin,
Spilled across the earth—slithering,
crawling into the fissures of a world undone.
The sun, a jaundiced specter, withered and died,
Its corpse suspended in the weightless air,
Where smoke unfurled like spectral hands,
Reaching, twisting around the bitter scent of ash,
And the sour exhalation
of greed's insatiable hunger.

We heard it before we saw it—
A soundless thunder that pressed against our hearts,
Crushing ribs and grinding teeth to powder,
Until the very air turned to glass,
Shattering with a whisper that slid through our skin:
"They come."

They rose, their heads endless,
Twisting like serpents in eternal dance,
Like roots that poisoned the well of the earth itself.
Their eyes—whirlpool abyssal pools,
Reflecting the ruin of every soul they consumed.
Their necks, knotted with ancient, unholy sin,
Slick with the grease of insatiable hunger.
Their wings—great black veils—
dragged the sun into nothingness,
Swallowing the light, devouring it whole.

Their mouths spilled rivers of molten lies:
"You made us, and we shall feast.
Your hands fed the fire.
Your silence stoked the flames."

Every step shattered mountains,
Rivers turned to steam at their touch.
Fields turned to ash, cities to dust.
And the people, the many,
Stood with mouths of ash

and eyes of despair,
Watching in silent agony
as the Hydra fed.

For it was we who gave them life—
We, the architects of ash, the weavers of sorrow's cloth.
From our marrow, we built their spires,
And raised their thrones upon the shattered
backs of the broken.

We called their fire "progress,"
And their hunger "the price of illumination."
And still,
Still, we bent our knees,
Still, we whispered the hollow word "fate,"
As the gods we forged gnawed
upon the bones of our hope.

But in the fissures of this dying earth,
Something stirred—
A breath,
faint as
the whisper
of dead winds
in a forgotten graveyard,
But growing, swelling:
"No more."

The Hydra turned,
Its heads unfurling
like the writhing tendrils of a cursed tree,
Each neck reaching toward the heavens,
Its mouths dripping with the venom
of ancient rot.
A thousand voices—
Thundering, unholy—
Chimed in discord, an endless dirge:

"You cannot fight.
You cannot win.
Your world spins on my wheel of hunger.
Your skies crumble,
devoured by the very fire you lit."

And yet,
Amidst the ruins, we stood.
Our hands raw, our breath shallow,
Chains dangling
at our sides,
Rusted but unbroken.
No swords to wield,
Only the shattered remnants
of our despair:
Plows turned to shields,
Shovels warped into battering rams.

A mother raised her hands,
blistered and bloodied,
Her child's ashes clinging
like ghosts to her skin.
And from our mouths,
blackened with the soot of our sins,
We spoke the word: "Enough."

The Hydra struck first,
Its breath a furnace,
molten with stolen light,
A conflagration that shattered stone,
that tore bone from sinew.
"You starve without me.
You cannot breathe without my fire."

But its coil met the hammer's blow,
And the first head fell,
Spilling black ichor—
Tar-thick, choked with decay,
Its fumes rising like a dirge
for the dead.
Yet still,
the Hydra writhed.
For every head severed,
two more emerged,

Like twisted roots from a poisoned well:
"Oil!" one hissed,
"Gold!" the other bellowed,
And the chorus rose—
A symphony
of insatiable hunger,
Each note a scream
of ravenous greed.

But we stood,
Our bodies blackened by smoke,
Our lungs choked with ash
that blotted out the stars.
We swung again,
And again,
Until the world trembled
beneath the weight of our defiance.

The Hydra faltered,
Its massive form heaving,
Its countless mouths gagging
on the ichor
of its own corruption.
The earth trembled beneath its weight,
And the sun—pale as bone,

A distant, dying eye—
Peeled through the choking haze.

It was not victory.
It was not peace.
But defiance—
Sharp and fleeting
as the edge of a blade,
A flicker of light
in the endless dark.

Yet even as the Hydra stumbled,
Its whispers clung to the air,
Seeping into the very soil,
Taking root in the fractures of a fractured world:
"You think you've won?
I do not die.
I wait."

For the Hydra's roots are countless,
And its heads, born of man's own making.
It sleeps in the vaults of power,
In the counting-houses of greed,
In the oil-slick seas and glittering towers.
As long as gold burns brighter than the sun,
As long as chains are forged in shadowed corners,
The Hydra will rise again,
And feast upon the soul of the world.

But now—
Now, the many have risen,
The spark has caught fire,
And though the Hydra slumbers,
Its dreams are watched,
Bound in the eyes of those who dare defy.

"Do not let it rise.
Do not let it feast."

The people turned from the ashes,
Their chains rusted but unbroken,
Their fists clenched,
Not in surrender,
but in the iron promise
of rebellion.

The Hydra sleeps.
For now.

SAD SONGS FROM AN OLD GOTH IN A TREE

20

HUMMING IN THE ASHES

Under a sepia sky,
where ravens echo old refrains,
the winds carry murmurs
of ages weighed by chains.
Shadows of towers crumble
into dust so fine,
while seeds of tomorrow's forests
wait, patient in their line.
We've watched masked hierarchs
whisper edicts to the blind,
their ledgers inked in crimson truths
that sear the mind.
Beneath the glare of neon lies,
so many souls grew numb,
yet humble roots beneath cracked pavement
now softly hum.
A sage once warned of painted screens
that hold us in a trance,
now fragments of those hollowed myths

blow free in winds of chance.
Where carbon ghosts and profit's tongue
once ruled the fading light,
a tender green assertion
breaks the silent, weary night.
Humming in the ashes of the West,
we breathe anew,
where quiet fields remember
all that empire threw.
The current hums with whispered hope
in wires underground,
from rusted dreams and hollow halls,
new beauty now is found.
In canopies of solar leaves,
the gentle morning gleams,
a different music flows
along regenerative streams.
We cradle fragile sparks that glow
beneath the old world's scorn,
where logic's hand and caring hearts
shape what can be reborn.
No more the hollow spectacle
of gilded lies on air,
but slow-grown trust in living systems,
delicate and fair.
As raven wings fade into green,
and pain dissolves to dew,
the murmured songs of distant minds
guide what we must renew.
Humming in the ashes of the West,
we breathe anew,

where soft moss climbs where borders fell,
and truths slip through.
The hum of solar whispers dance
in subtle vines of grace,
from broken crowns and corporate tombs,
we shape a kinder place.
Under gardens blooming in the hum
of gentle sun,
we dream beyond the pale charade
that once weighed a world undone.
In each bright leaf and cobalt cell,
a treaty with the Earth,
no heavy crowns, no iron words,
just honesty and worth.
Humming in the ashes of the West,
we bloom and grow,
no tyrant's laugh can snuff the green
or stop the gentle flow.
By shifting sands and whispered minds,
the future's softly spun,
in emerald shoots, in earnest hands,
a brighter age is won.
Let old ghosts cry their hollow dirge,
we have no debt to pay,
the rising sun of gentler worlds
will wash their smoke away.
We hum in quiet symphonies
of seeds beneath each crest,
as new empires of kindness rise,
and all may finally rest.

21
SWAN SONG

Under black lights, in the roar of the crowd,
We danced like gods, too young, too loud.
Spinning in chaos, a fever dream,
Bodies like stars in a cosmic scream.

The music hit hard, the nights hit harder,
We burned through the edge, we couldn't go farther.
But we never cared, we were infinite then,
Until the dawn called us back again.

This is my swan song, my final refrain,
A love letter carved in pleasure and pain.
The party is over, the lights come on,
But I'll play this last song before I'm gone.

Some stayed young, beautiful, and gone,
Some lived long enough to watch it all go wrong.

We shared a train through a starry night,
Got off at stops, lost in the light.

Now I'm deaf from the screams, lost in the glow,
Chasing the echoes of a feeling long ago.
Mixing the noise, with ears torn apart,
Creating for ghosts, with a broken heart.

This is my swan song, my final refrain,
A love letter carved in pleasure and pain.
The dancefloor is empty, the crowd's moved on,
But I'll sing this last song before I'm gone.

Do you remember the heat, the sweat, the sound?
Do you remember the way we spun around?
We were one, for a moment, alive and whole,
Now we're fragments, shadows, drifting souls.

This is my swan song, my fading cry,
A love letter to the nights we flew so high.
The music is fading, the fire is gone,
But I'll give it my all, one last song.

Left alone with echoes, ghosts in my mind,
I mix down the memories we left behind.

And though you don't hear me, though no one stays,
I'll play this swan song anyway.

ABOUT THE AUTHOR

Jorah Kai's life blends adventure and creativity, with passions spanning martial arts, music, technology, travel, food, philosophy, revelry, gaming, and writing. After headlining festivals as a DJ and producer, he embraced the gonzo journalism spirit, leading him to cyberpunk Chongqing in 2014. There, he teaches English and art history while writing for *iChongqing*, capturing stories of a changing world.

During the pandemic, Kai made his mark as the first Canadian journalist in China to report for *CTV News*, gaining recognition for his prescient predictions. His nonfiction works, like *Kai's Diary*, *The Invisible War*, *Year of the Rat*, and *Aye of the Tiger* explore existentialism, crisis, and absurdity. His debut novel, *Amos the Amazing*, became an international children's steampunk and solarpunk bestseller, and his literary-horror work *The Sun Also Rises on Cthulhu* further expands his range.

Now, with *Sad Songs from an Old Goth in a Tree*, Kai returns to his roots, blending poetry and music into a haunting collection, paired with the album by the same name and *Voidwalker*.

His writing, cinematic and immersive, captures the human condition with vivid clarity.

Kai writes on beaches around the world, enjoys the sea, and when not stationary, he's often on wheels. Discover more at jorahkai.com.

OTHER BOOKS BY JORAH KAI

阿莫斯的奇幻世界

Amos the Amazing,
Aye of the Tiger

凯哥的日记

Kai's Diary
Lobster Revolution
The Invisible War
The Sun Also Rises on Cthulhu
The Year of the Rat